"Picking out a faint planet amid the myriads of star images would be literally like finding a needle in a haystack."

— **Clyde W. Tombaugh, 1980**

Our remarkable children will inherit the world we have created, and build a better one for all with the knowledge and experience they have gained. I hope my role as author and storyteller will have added something of value.

Diane Phelps Budden

For my shining stars - Kevin, Izzi, and Zoe.

Tanja Bauerle

Needle in a Haystack: How Clyde W. Tombaugh Found an Awesome New World
Includes bibliographic references

ISBN: 979-8-218-26529-8

Red Rock Mountain Press
Sedona, Arizona
www.dianephelpsbudden.com

NEEDLE IN A HAYSTACK

HOW CLYDE W. TOMBAUGH FOUND AN AWESOME NEW WORLD

WRITTEN BY
DIANE PHELPS BUDDEN

DESIGN AND LAYOUT BY
TANJA BAUERLE

Red Rock Mountain Press, LLC.

Clyde's favorite planets as a boy were Mars and Jupiter. He became fascinated by planet Jupiter. It led to his interest in building a telescope to study the planet better so he could make drawings of its surface.

The stars lit up the night like birthday candles on a cake. Clyde focused the telescope on the moon, pale yellow like a big melon. It looked close enough to touch.

"Clyde," his father said, "look at Mars! You can see the polar cap."

Clyde's family posed for this photo on the Locust Dell Farm combine used to harvest wheat. His mother Adella is to his left, and father Muron next to her.

Clyde W. Tombaugh

His father and Uncle Lee taught him everything they knew about planets. They shared a telescope bought from the 1919 Sears, Roebuck & Company catalog. Uncle Lee was an amateur astronomer and loaned him an astronomy book. Clyde read it until he knew it by heart.

"Clyde sure loves the stars," said his brother Roy.

Clyde helped his father on the family farm. "I started milking cows when I was 8 years old," Clyde said. He could plant corn and cut oats and wheat. He drove the threshing machine that separated the wheat from its husk. He liked to care for the farm animals, especially Old Doll who pulled the plow.

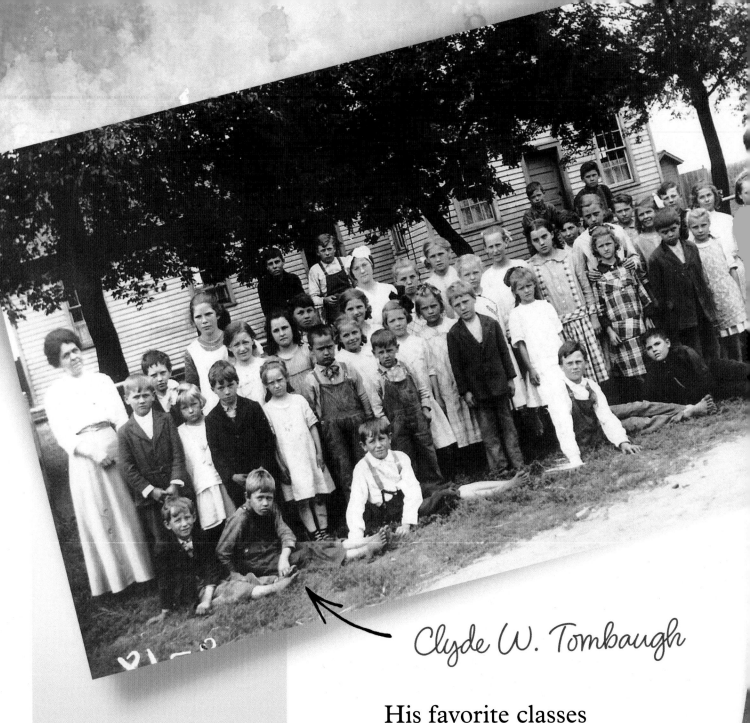

Clyde W. Tombaugh

Clyde's family lived in Streator, Illinois, before moving to Kansas. Clyde attended Heenanville School outside Streator. It was a typical country school with children divided into two classrooms by grade. This photo was taken in 1915 when Clyde was about eight years old.

His favorite classes at school were geography and history. His fifth-grade teacher showed him how to draw maps.

What does the surface of Mars and Jupiter look like?

Clyde W. Tombaugh

Clyde was a member of the Burdett High School track team in Burdett, Kansas. In a 1924 track meet he placed second in high jump and third in pole vault. The principal said that Clyde was trying "to get nearer to his beloved stars." Clyde graduated in 1925.

Clyde read everything he could find about astronomy. He learned about Lowell Observatory in Flagstaff, Arizona. It was built by Percival Lowell who was a self-taught astronomer.

I want to be an astronomer too!

Lowell's campus in 1928 included the administrative building with offices for three astronomers. The Lawrence Lowell Telescope was housed in a newly built dome a short way behind the building. To the left are a few astronomy books that Clyde read as a teenager.

The Pith of Astronomy

Mars and its Mysteries

The True Story of the Man in the Moon

Percival Lowell founded Lowell Observatory in 1894 to study the planets. He spent 13 years in the search for Planet X. He asked the observatory staff to continue the search after he died. This photo shows him viewing the planet Venus during the daytime.

At night he used the telescope to study Mars and Jupiter and carefully draw their surfaces. He taught his younger brothers and sister to use the telescope.

"No matter how hard he works during the day," said his brother, "at night he stays up to study the sky."

Robert Tombaugh was Clyde's younger brother.
The drawings to the right were some of the first Clyde did of Jupiter.

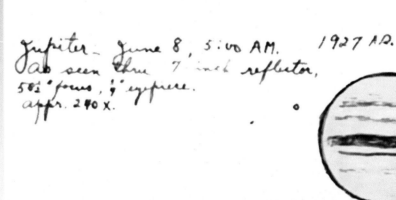

Jupiter - June 8, 5:00 AM. 1927 A.D.
As seen thru 7-inch reflector, 58½° focus, ¼" eyepiece. appr. 240 X.

Jupiter - Aug. 4, 1927. at 4:00 A M
As seen thru 7-inch reflector, 240 X.

Ask any questions you wish about the contents of this page. They will be gladly answered.

THE COMPANION — FOR ALL THE FAMILY

BOYS' PAGE for NOVEMBER

November 14, 1918

Address your letters to THE EDITOR OF THE BOYS' PAGE, THE YOUTH'S COMPANION, BOSTON, MASS

WHO "WRIT" FOR YOU TO COME?

CONTRARY to custom, Mr. Benjamin Blair, sinew, brain and inspiration of the great Middle Western mercantile house, came to his office at half past eight instead of nine o'clock. None of the general office force knew that he was already in his private room at the time of their arrival.

As he pored over the outspread sheets of figures on his desk, he was half aware of varied comments of the clerks as they entered the adjoining room. "From one it was a curt, "Morning!" from her, "Fine day!" in a tone that showed a good breakfast. But when at words at once caught the attention of the beginning to late this room!" Grant had the company only five days. "Nothing driven civil! Stoods hard as a brickbat; filing all day. Any cub can do that! The boss'll this job very long...

[remainder of story column largely illegible]

A CYLINDER STAR MAP

CAN you name the bright stars that are visible this evening? Flat star maps are not easy to use, and globes are expensive; but, by following carefully the directions given here, it is a simple matter to make a good substitute for a globe. This cylinder star map is an original device. The Editor of the Boys' Page believes that it has never before been described in print.

A large cylindrical paste-board carton, the taller the better, is the necessary foundation. Draw a circle the size of the end of the carton, and divide it into twenty-four parts. An easy way to do it is to lay a watch in the centre of the circle and mark off points for the twelve hours; then insert halfway points. Divide one of the rays thus drawn into four equal parts and draw the three concentric circles shown in Fig. 1.

The circles represent distances of ten, twenty, thirty and forty degrees from the Pole Star, and the rays show how much of the firmament seems to turn in each of the twenty-four hours of the day. By the aid of the lines copy the constellations, Cassiopeia's Chair, the Big Dipper and the Little Dipper, shown in Fig. 1.

Then cut out the outer circle and paste it on the end of the cylinder. Next, wrap a sheet of drawing paper round the carton and mark where each of the twenty-four rays meets the upper edge of it—the line P Q in Fig. 2. Flatten out the paper, and rule the twenty-five vertical lines shown in Fig. 2, the twenty-fifth of which, at P, should fit the first, at Q, when you paste the rectangle on the carton. Then draw the horizontal lines that, like the circles in Fig. 1, represent intervals of ten degrees of distance from the Pole Star.

The equator should be represented by a heavier line, or by one of a different color. By the help of the two sets of lines, copy the stars and their names and everything in Fig 2 with the following exceptions: omit the "horizon" (the curved line of dashes), the large letters E, N, W, S, and the strip of time labels between the line X Y and the line through Alchernar.

Before you paste the rectangle on the carton, cut out a rectangle of similar size from extra stout paper, and trim it so that its upper boundary will follow the curved line of dashes and its lower edge will be the line X Y. This piece will be called the shield. On the shield paste the things in Fig. 2 that you omitted from the rectangle, and also the portion of the equator line from E to W.

Now paste the rectangle on the carton, taking care that the lines at P and Q come together opposite the end of the ray marked with the arrow in Fig. 1. Then wrap the shield round the carton (not too tightly), and paste the end E X to the flap at the other end. If you can slip the shield round freely on the

[continues]

your star map is now ready for use. You find it accurate enough if you live in latitudes between 35° N and 45° N. If you live as far south set the curve on the shield so that it reaches square lower at 8 and correspondingly higher in order to take in Algol and its mate. adjust the indicator, pick out the time of day shield and the time of the year on the cylinder bring them into coincidence... below the horizon are now hid the rest are shown

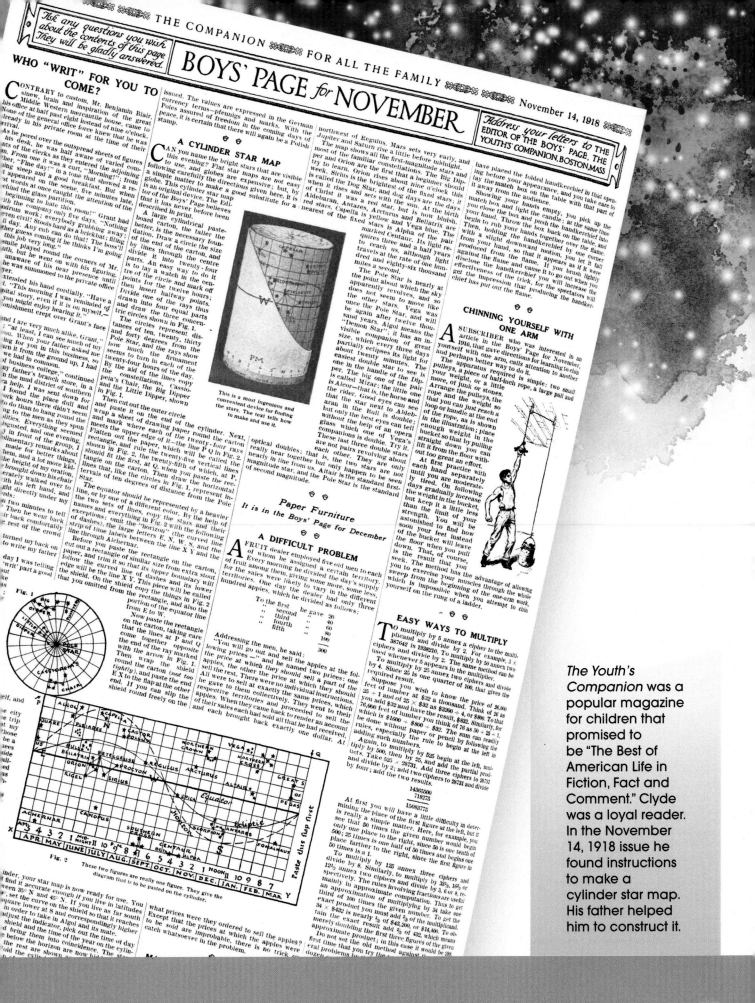

Caption: This is a most ingenious and convenient device for finding the stars. The text tells how to make and use it.

(figure labels, Fig. 1: BIG DIPPER, LITTLE DIPPER, POLE STAR, CASSIOPEIA'S CHAIR)

(figure labels, Fig. 2: ALGOL, CAPELLA, PLEIADES, N, CASTOR, POLLUX, BULL, BELLATRIX, BETELGEUSE, ORION, RIGEL, SIRIUS, PROCYON, REGULUS, ARCTURUS, SPICA, VEGA, NORTHERN CROWN, NORTHERN CROSS, ALTAIR, GREAT SQUARE OF PEGASUS, ECLIPTIC, ANTARES, SCORPION, CENTAUR, ALPHA BETA, $, FOMALHAUT, ACHERNAR, CANOPUS, SOUTHERN CROSS, Equator, Horizon; APR MAY JUNE JULY AUG SEPT OCT NOV DEC JAN FEB MAR; Paste this flap first)*

These two figures are really one figure. They give the diagram that is to be pasted on the cylinder.

Paper Furniture

It is in the Boys' Page for December

A DIFFICULT PROBLEM

A FRUIT dealer employed five old men to each of whom he assigned a certain territory. Every morning he divided the day's supply of fruit among them, giving some more, some less, for the sales were likely to vary in the different territories. One day the dealer had only three hundred apples, which he divided as follows:

To the first	he gave	20
" second		40
" third		60
" fourth		80
" fifth		100
		300

Addressing the men, he said: "You will go out and sell the apples at the following prices —, and he named two prices: one the price at which they should sell a part of the apples, the other the price at which they should sell the rest. There were no individual instructions. All were to sell at exactly the same prices, which he gave to them collectively. They went to their respective territories and proceeded to sell the apples. When they came back to render an account of their sales each had sold all that he had received, and each brought back exactly one dollar.

At first you will have a little difficulty in determining the place of the first figure at the left, but it is really a simple matter. Here, for example, you see that 50 times the given number would begin only one place to the right, since 50 is one tenth of 500; 25 times is one half of 50 times and begins one place farther to the right, since the first figure in 50 times is a 1...

what prices were they ordered to sell the apples? Except that the prices at which the apples were to be sold are improbable, there is no trick to catch whatsoever in the problem.

A CYLINDER STAR MAP *(continued top of page)*

[northwest of Regulus. Mars sets very early, and this evening.] Jupiter and Saturn rise a little before midnight. The map shows all the first-magnitude stars and most of the familiar constellations. The Big Dipper and Orion are the first that a beginner should try to learn. Orion rises about nine o'clock this week. Sirius is the brightest of the fixed stars; it is called the Dog Star, and dog days are the days when it rises and sets with the sun. At the birth of Christ it was a red star, but is now bluish. Aldebaran, Antares, Arcturus and Bellatrix are red stars; Capella is yellow and Vega blue. The nearest of the fixed stars is Alpha of the pair marked Centaur. Its light requires three and a half years to reach us, although light travels at the rate of one hundred and eighty-six thousand miles a second.

The Pole Star is nearly at the point about which the sky apparently revolves, and does not seem to move like the other stars. Vega will once the Pole Star, and will be again after twelve thousand years. Algol means the "Demon Star", it has an invisible companion of great size, which every three days partially eclipses its light for about twenty minutes. The easiest double star to see is one in the handle of the Dipper. The big one of the pair is called Mizar; the little one is Alcor—that is, the horse and the rider. Good eyes can see that the star next to Aldebaran in the Bull is double; but only the best eyes can tell without the help of an opera glass, which one of Vega's companions is double. Try it. These last three double stars are not pairs revolving about each other. They are only really near together but only happen to be nearly in line from us. Altair is the standard first-magnitude star, and the Pole Star is the standard of second magnitude.

CHINNING YOURSELF WITH ONE ARM

A SUBSCRIBER who was interested in an article in the Boys' Page for November, 1916, that gave directions for learning to chin yourself with one arm, calls attention to another and perhaps better way to do it.

The apparatus required is simple: two small pulleys, a piece of half-inch rope, a large pail and more, of junk or stones. Arrange the pulleys, the rope and the weight so that you can just reach a loop or handle at the end of the rope, as is shown in the illustration; place enough weight in the bucket so that by pulling straight down you can lift it from the floor without too great an effort.

At first practice with each hand separately until you are moderately tired. On following days gradually increase the weight in the bucket, but keep it a little less than the limit of your strength. You will be astonished to find how soon your feet instead of the bucket will leave the floor when you pull down. That, of course, is the result that you seek. The method has the advantage of allowing you to exercise your muscles through the whole sweep from the beginning of the one-arm work, which is impossible when you attempt to chin yourself on the rung of a ladder.

EASY WAYS TO MULTIPLY

TO multiply by 5 annex a cipher to the multiplicand and divide by 2. For example, 387642 is 1938210. To multiply by 50 annex two ciphers and divide by 2. The same method can be used whenever 5 appears in the multiplier.

To multiply by 25 annex two ciphers and divide by 4. Since 25 is one quarter of 100, that gives the required result.

Suppose you wish to know the price of 26,000 feet of lumber at $32 a thousand. Think of 26 as 25 + 1 and of 25 × 32 as $800 ÷ 4, or $80. That is, you add $32 and have the result, $832. Similarly, for 76,000 feet of lumber you think of 76 as 50 + 25 + 1, which is $1600 + $800 + $32. The sum can readily be done without paper or pencil by following the rules, especially the rule to begin at the left in adding such numbers.

Again, to multiply by 525 begin at the left, multiply by 500, then by 25, and add the partial product. Take 525 × 28531. Add three ciphers to 28531 and divide by 2; add two ciphers to 28531 and divide by four; add the two results.

$$14365500$$
$$718275$$

$$15083775$$

To multiply by 125 annex three ciphers and divide by 8. Similarly, to multiply by 33⅓, 16⅔ or 12½ annex two ciphers and divide by 3, 6 or 8, respectively. The rules involving fractions are useful mainly in approximate computation. Thus to get an approximation of ⅓ of 100 times the given number. To get the exact product you must add ⅔ of the multiplicand. 34 × $432 is nearly ½ of $43,200, or $14,400. To obtain the exact result add ⅔ of 432, which means merely doubling the first three figures of the given approximate product; in this case it would be 28...

Do not test the old method against the first time that you try the several problems...

Clyde made this telescope in 1928 with parts from a 1910 Buick automobile and a mounting made from farm machinery. Director Dr. V. M. Slipher at Lowell Observatory was so impressed by the telescope and Clyde's drawings of Jupiter that he offered him a job at the observatory to search for a new planet. Clyde's telescope can be viewed today at Lowell Observatory.

Clyde on the family farm with his new telescope.

Clyde built a better telescope following the instructions in a science magazine. He used parts from farm machinery and a 1910 Buick automobile.

One day a huge storm with black thunderclouds and dazzling lightning rained hailstones as big as walnuts, destroying the wheat and oats. His money for college was gone. He wanted a job that didn't depend on the weather.

I have to leave the farm. Can I work as an astronomer without a college degree?

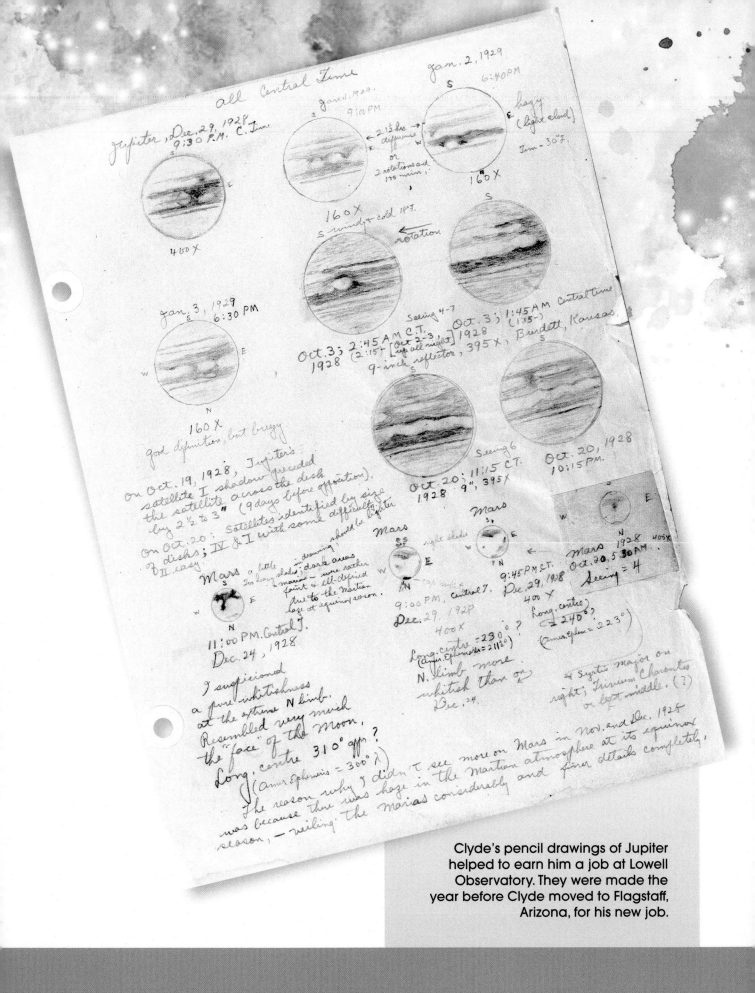

Clyde's pencil drawings of Jupiter helped to earn him a job at Lowell Observatory. They were made the year before Clyde moved to Flagstaff, Arizona, for his new job.

Dr. V.M. Slipher was an experienced astronomer and Director of Lowell Observatory after Percival Lowell passed away. He was known for research that led to the theory of the expanding universe. In order to continue Lowell's search for a new planet he obtained funds to build a new telescope and hired Clyde to operate it.

He mailed the drawings of Mars and Jupiter to the Lowell Observatory director Dr. V. M. Slipher. The observatory was looking for an amateur astronomer willing to work long hours for little pay to search for a new planet. Percival Lowell was his hero. He had been searching beyond Neptune for Planet X before he died.

"I'm impressed with your drawings and excellent homemade telescope," said Dr. Slipher. "I hope you will come to Arizona to help us."

"HA! I'm going to be an astronomer!" Clyde said to his parents.

Clyde was excited to be going to Lowell Observatory, but felt sad when he boarded the train to Flagstaff. When will I see my family again?

"It's important for you to pursue your dream of becoming an astronomer," his father said.

"I think your opportunities there will be wonderful," said his mother. "Let me know if you need extra covers for your bed."

The beautiful San Francisco Peaks dominate the skyline in Flagstaff just as they did when Clyde lived there.

Back row, left to right: Brothers
Robert, Roy, Mr. Muron Tombaugh,
Clyde and Brother Charles.
Bottom row is sister Anita and Mrs.
Adella Tombaugh. Clyde was 35
years old.

When he arrived at Lowell Observatory in the winter of 1929 Clyde cleaned floors and filled the furnace. He showed visitors how the telescope worked. On snowy days he shoveled the roofs of the buildings.

The observatory had purchased a new telescope that could be used to photograph the sky too. Clyde helped Dr. Slipher set it up. A new dome was built to house it.

He spent all his time in the dome where the telescope was located. In winter when the dome shutters were open, a bitter cold crept into his bones. He often worked late into the night. His eyes were sore and he was sleepy.

I'm glad I have the night sky for company. It's not so lonely in the dark when you know the names of the stars.

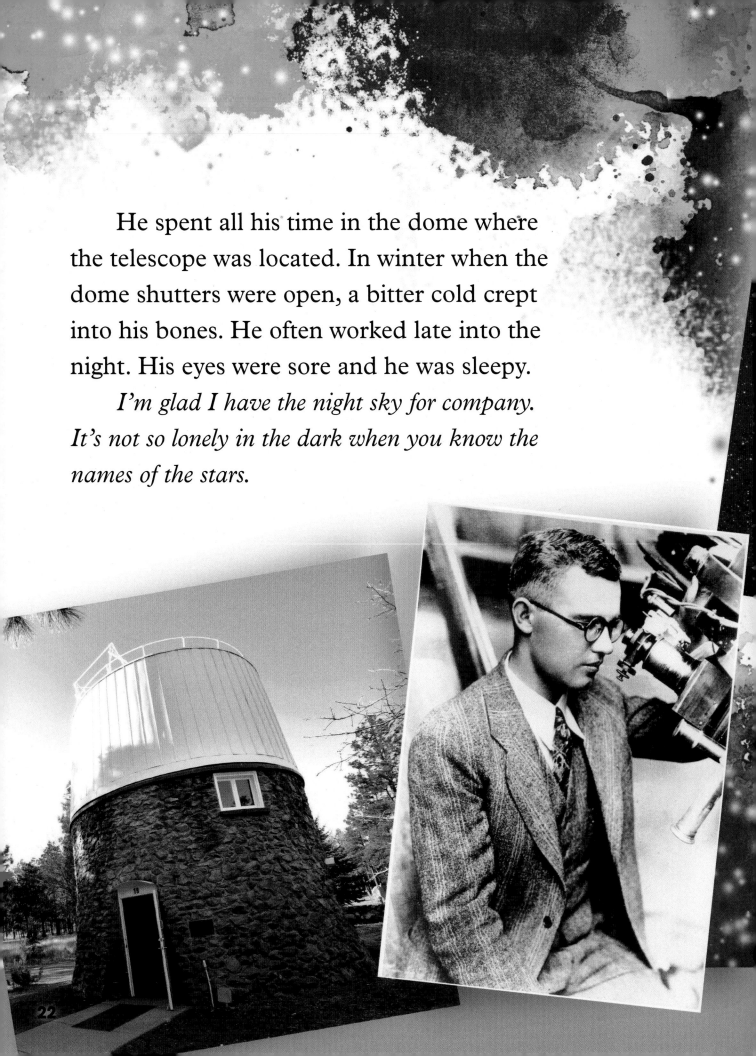

Clyde took these photos of the great star cloud of Sagittarius and the belt and sword of Orion in the Milky Way galaxy. He searched for the new planet in these constellations and many others. Each tiny star image was a candidate for a planet. "In a good day's work, I examined 30,000-60,000 star images," said Clyde.

Purchased and built by Lowell
Observatory to find a new planet, the
Lawrence Lowell telescope could also
take photographs. A new dome was
built to house it. The unheated dome
would prove to be Clyde's principal
workplace for more than 10 years.

One night it was so cold he felt drowsy and dreamy. Do I have hypothermia? Is my body temperature too low? He stood up and ran around the telescope to warm up his fingers and toes. It was a close call, like the night a growling mountain lion circled the dome. His heart was thumping as he raced back to his room.

Mountain Lions roam Arizona, usually at dawn or dusk. Clyde encountered one circling the dome while he was at work searching for Pluto.

Clyde wrote letters to his parents to keep them up-to-date on his search. "Thanks for the biscuits, ma. How is everyone there? Is Old Doll still feeling peppy?" he wrote. "I often think of the dear old horse."

He told them about a visiting astronomer who had looked at his photos. He told me I was wasting my time, "All the planets have been discovered."

I don't believe him and I won't stop until I prove him wrong.

Clyde and his family exchanged many letters from the time he arrived at Lowell Observatory until Pluto's discovery. His father Muron "pictured" his farm chores in these drawings, "Dad Doing his Daily Dozen," and sent them to Clyde.

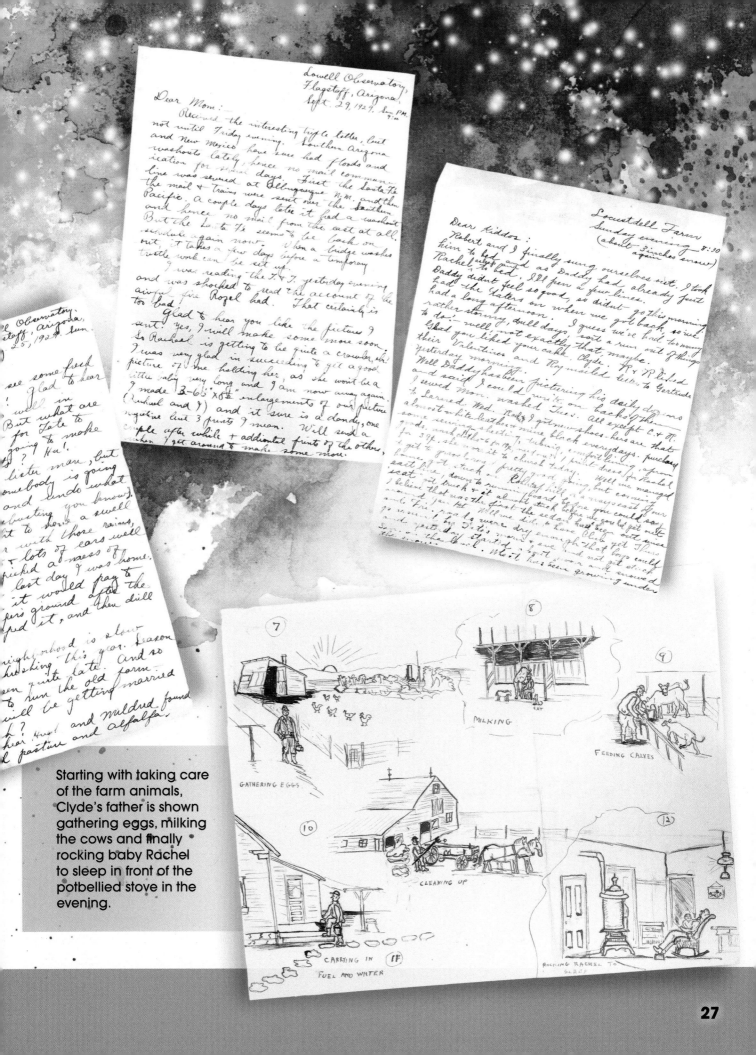

Starting with taking care of the farm animals, Clyde's father is shown gathering eggs, milking the cows and finally rocking baby Rachel to sleep in front of the potbellied stove in the evening.

Clyde took hundreds of photos of millions of stars. Dr. Slipher asked him to examine each one carefully. He compared photos taken on different days in the Blink machine.

Blink! Blink!

Clyde used a blink machine to reveal the location of a new planet.

He was looking for distant movement of points of light that might mean a new planet. Stars didn't change position in the sky. He tracked all his findings in a logbook.

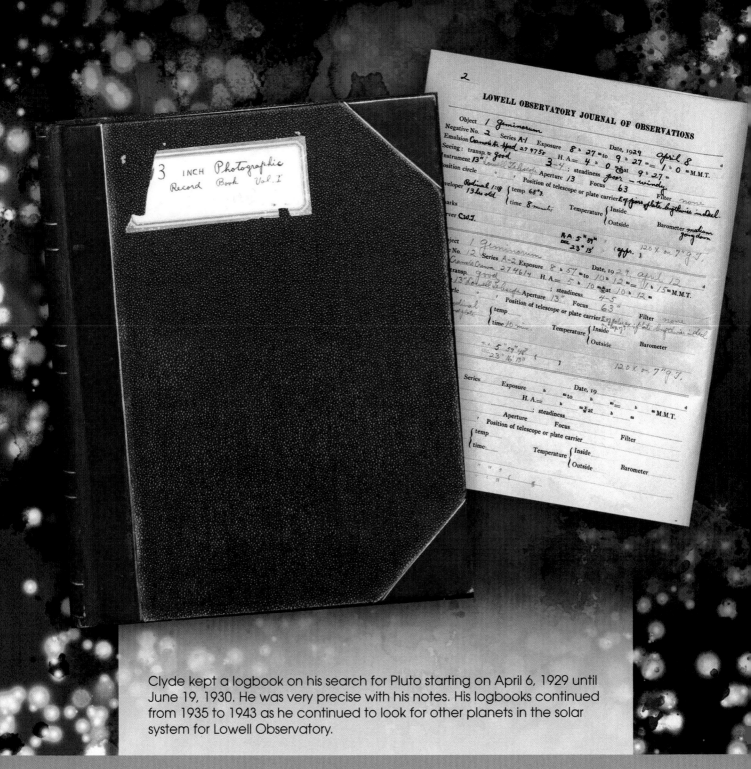

Clyde kept a logbook on his search for Pluto starting on April 6, 1929 until June 19, 1930. He was very precise with his notes. His logbooks continued from 1935 to 1943 as he continued to look for other planets in the solar system for Lowell Observatory.

31

It was like looking for a needle in a haystack.

Position of Pluto

January 23, 1930

Clyde used the Blink machine to compare photos taken on different days. These two photos taken on January 23, 1930 and January 30, 1930 show that an object has moved its position in the sky. (See the arrows.)

New position of Pluto

January 30, 1930

Clyde suspected he had indeed discovered a new planet! He estimated he spent 7,000 hours using the blink machine, and several thousand hours taking photos in a search for the new planet.

HA! One of the spots was in a new position! He had butterflies in his stomach, like when he rode the Ferris Wheel at the county fair. He gathered the photos and hurried to Dr. Slipher's office.

"I've found the planet," he said. It was February 18, 1930. He had been searching for 300 days.

"We'll have to check these photos carefully," said Dr. Slipher. "I don't want to tell the world about the new planet until we're sure."

"It was a strange flicker of starlight in a routine day's work. Am I excited? You bet," said Clyde.

"Dr. Slipher, I've found the planet,"
Clyde said.
It was February 18, 1930.

Clyde ate at the Black Cat Café in Flagstaff many evenings. On the day he discovered the new planet he was very nervous waiting to hear from Dr. Slipher about his discovery. He went to eat at the café and attend a movie around the corner.

Clyde wanted to tell his family. He was so excited he couldn't sleep and went to town to have dinner at the Black Cat Café. The butterflies were still fluttering so he walked to the Orpheum to see a popular movie.

The staff of Lowell Observatory in 1930 included: Clyde in the front row, far left; Dr. Slipher is second from the right; Slipher's brother E.C. Slipher who also worked at the observatory in the back row, far right. (He was known for his Mars research); C.O. Lampland at left of Slipher in the back row worked with Percival Lowell in the search for Planet X.

Early in March Dr. Slipher announced the new planet to the world, the first one discovered by an American. Newspaper headlines shouted the story of Clyde and his planet, "Ninth Planet Discovered on Edge of Solar System; First Found in 84 Years."

Lowell Observatory had a professional photo taken of Clyde by Fronsky Sudios in Flagstaff in the early 1930s to accompany newspaper stories, books and other publications.

He and the other astronomers at Lowell Observatory couldn't believe the hullabaloo. Overnight he was famous. People in town stopped Clyde in the street to congratulate him. Hundreds of people across the country sent letters.

Lowell Observatory received an avalanche of letters and telegrams from the public when Pluto was announced. Many wrote to suggest a name. Scientists and observatories from around the world sent messages asking for more information and congratulating the observatory.

The telegram below was sent to Clyde from his proud parents.

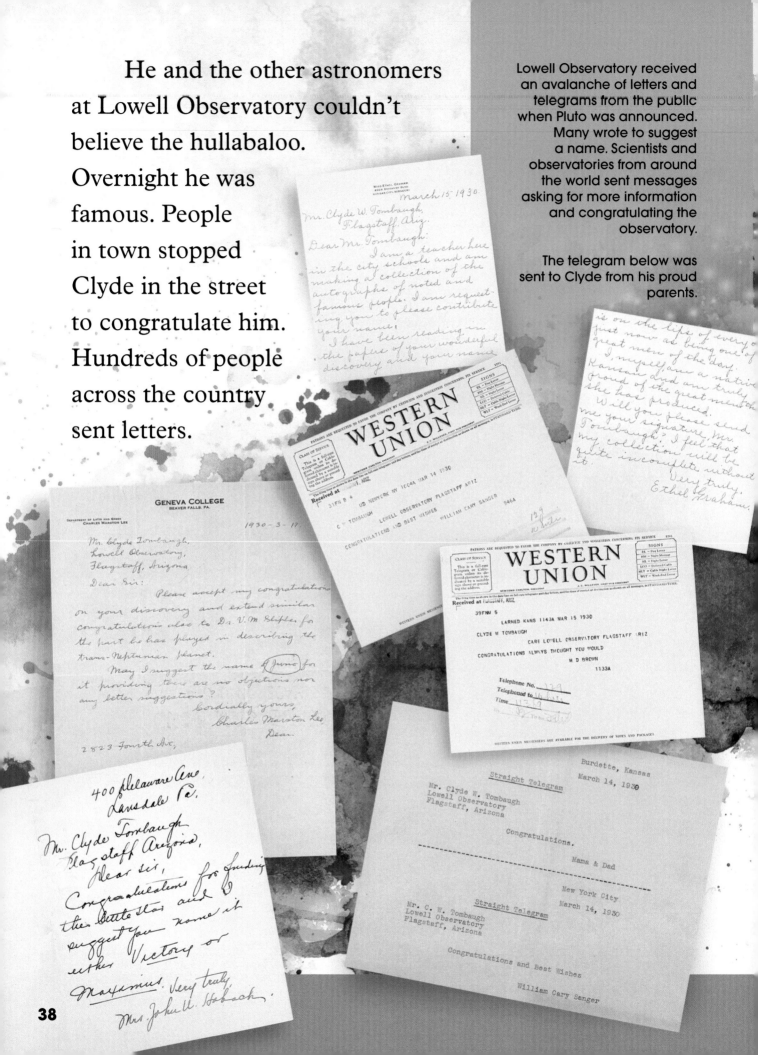

5 AU D 21 RCA –

OXFORD MAR 16

WLT–

LOWELL OBSERVATORY

FLAGSTAFF ARIZ.

NAMING NEW PLANET PLEASE CONSIDER PLUTO , SUGGESTED BY SMALL
GIRL . VEBTIA NUBNEY , FOR DARK GLOOMY PLANET .

545 PM   TURNER .

Venetia Burney was an eleven-year-old-girl from Oxford, England. She had been learning about mythology in school and thought that Pluto, the god of the Greek underworld, might be a good choice. Her grandfather told a British astronomer who telegrammed the suggestion to Lowell Observatory.

The public wanted to know the name of the new planet. Venetia Burney, an eleven-year-old girl in England, suggested Pluto. The observatory wanted the name to fit the Greek and Roman names of the other planets so they chose Pluto.

Clyde became well known when he discovered Pluto. He was the third person in the world to officially find a planet, and the only American. He continued to look for other planets at Lowell Observatory for another ten years.

HA! He had proven the other astronomers wrong. It might not be Percival Lowell's Planet X, but the youngest astronomer at the observatory found a new planet.

"I guess my kid sister sized me up right," said Clyde. "She thinks I discovered a whole new world. I guess I did. How would you feel if you saw a new world giving you the high sign?"

Clyde was often asked if there were more planets in the solar system. He searched ten more years at the observatory. He found almost 90 million objects in the sky and checked out thousands of possible planets. He knew future astronomers would continue looking with more powerful telescopes.

"I think there could be more planets beyond Pluto," Clyde said. "HA! It will be like looking for a needle in a haystack!"

Our solar system is part of the Milky Way and has eight planets circling the sun. Pluto is part of the Kuiper Belt outside the solar system, along with many icy orbs.

Neptune

Pluto

Saturn

Uranus

Mars

Jupiter

Venus

Earth

Mercury

Author's Notes

Writing the biography of Clyde W. Tombaugh has been an honor and a joy. I hoped to celebrate his perseverance and passion for astronomy, and the life lessons they provide. He was a farm boy without a college degree and very little funds who impressed a Lowell Observatory astronomer with his dedication to detail and ability to educate himself about astronomy.

Lowell Observatory Director V. M. Slipher knew that Clyde was the right person at the right time to find a new planet. This kind of opportunity might await anyone with the tenacity of Clyde W. Tombaugh to reach their goals.

Clyde had a king-sized sense of humor! HA! He created many puns (using words with two or more meanings). My favorites are the "crow" puns:

Question: When a crow goes crazy what is he called?

Answer: A raven maniac

Question: What kind of needlework does Mrs. Crow do?
Answer: Crochet

I hope this book will build more interest in Pluto and New Horizons continuing journey across the universe. The mission has enriched our knowledge of the solar system and beyond.

I would be very happy if children who read my book would want to be a scientist or explorer.

Pluto has had a wide-ranging effect on the names of things. Started in 2013, Pluto TV was inspired by the "underdog" planet. In a 1930 cartoon the Disney Company named Mickey Mouse's new pet dog Pluto after the new-found planet. Element 94 in the Periodic Table, plutonium, was named after Pluto in 1941.

Kevin Schindler
Historian Kevin Schindler at Lowell Observatory viewing the sky using Clyde's boyhood telescope.

Acknowledgements

I could not have written this book without the help of Lowell Observatory's historian Kevin Schindler. He shared information and photos (and much time) from Lowell's archives about Clyde and the discovery of Pluto, and explained the technical aspects of astronomy and planet hunting. I am lucky to have this first-class observatory in my backyard. Clyde's son Alden Tombaugh brought his father alive for me (especially his great sense of humor).

Clyde gave his papers and photographs to the New Mexico State University Library (NMSU) in Las Cruces, New Mexico. Most of the material is digitized and easily accessed. The support from NMSU collections librarians was invaluable.

The NASA JPL site offers a treasure trove of information, freely available. See their photo collection to expand your understanding of the universe.

Like most books, this one has been years in the making. I am grateful to all my fellow writers, family and friends who encouraged me to stick with it.

Clyde W. Tombaugh, 1907-1997:
A Lifetime of Discovery

"In 1915 the first signs of a lifelong hobby began to creep into me. It was the study of astronomy. I was only in 4th grade."

Clyde at the door to the dome housing the telescope.

When Clyde W. Tombaugh discovered Pluto in 1930, he did not have a college degree. He was very excited when he found Pluto, but to become a real astronomer he needed a college degree. Winning a scholarship at the University of Kansas, he earned both a bachelor's and master's degree. He continued to work for Lowell Observatory for ten more years to search for other planets. After he earned his degrees he was hired by Arizona State Teacher's College in Flagstaff (now Northern Arizona University) to teach physics.

Clyde married Patsy Edson in 1934 and they had two children, Annette and Alden. In 1946 the family moved to Las Cruces, New Mexico. He worked at the White Sands Proving Ground until he transferred to New Mexico State University (NMSU) as a professor. He established a graduate astronomy program there. The school named its observatory after him.

Clyde and his wife Patsy and children Annette and Alden

Clyde retired in 1973 and wrote a book with Sir Patrick Moore about his discovery of Pluto titled Out of the Darkness: The Planet Pluto. He continued to build telescopes of varying strengths and sizes in his backyard. (He built over 30 telescopes in his lifetime.) He died in 1997 at the age of 90. It is estimated that he photographed over 75 per cent of the sky in his lifetime. He discovered one planet, one comet, 144 asteroids, and many stars and star clusters.

In retirement Clyde continued to use the telescope he built in 1928 in his backyard.

When NASA's New Horizons mission left earth in 2006 to fly by Pluto, a bit of Clyde's ashes made the journey. A plaque identified him as the man who discovered Pluto. Pluto's large heart-shaped area was named the Tombaugh Regio.

Clyde was known for his sense of humor and loved puns (using words with two or more meanings). He wrote this pun:

Question: What kind of bicycle are you riding?

Answer: One that's "too tired."

"HA! HA!" he might say if he thought the pun was funny and then slap his knee.

At Lowell Observatory the Pluto Walk ends at the dome housing the Lawrence Lowell (Pluto Discovery) Telescope and Clyde is honored with a bronze bust and plaque. On the annual anniversary of Pluto's discovery, Lowell has an "I Love Pluto" celebration. The 100th anniversary will be in 2030.

Clyde's pet cat Pluto.

Tiny Pluto Has a Big Heart!

Pluto is an icy round orb smaller than Earth's moon. It has five moons rotating around it. Charon, that is half the size of Pluto, has been re-classified as a satellite and is often considered a planet by planetary scientists.

Pluto's surface is very complex with icy mountains, volcanoes and glaciers. The ice is mostly frozen nitrogen gas, not water. Its air is very thin. If you weigh 100 pounds on earth, you will weigh 6.7 pounds on Pluto. Scientists think its rocky center gives off heat that may have created an ocean below the surface.

It takes 248 Earth years for Pluto to travel around the sun. That's over 88,000 days! It's a long trip. And a cold one. Pluto's minus 387-degree temperature is about a 450-degree difference from Earth! Pluto orbits beyond Neptune so its days are dim compared to Earth. Particles of Pluto's atmosphere become part of the ice, giving Pluto a yellow or pink color.

In 2006 the International Astronomical Union (IAU) decided that Pluto was not a planet, but a dwarf planet. Why? Well, many other icy planet-like orbs were found in the newly discovered Kuiper Belt outside the solar system. Scientists think Pluto is part of this region along with hundreds of other icy bodies.

Planets share the following characteristics:

1. They orbit the sun.
2. They are big enough to be a ball.
3. Their gravity cleared away any other objects of similar size near their orbit around the sun.

One of the first official close-up photos of Pluto taken by New Horizons shows the heart-shaped area that was named Tombaugh Regio in honor of Clyde. To the left of the area is a crater named for Venetia Burney. Not shown is an area beyond the Burney Crater named for Lowell Observatory.

Pluto meets the first two characteristics, but not the last one. It was downgraded to a dwarf planet much to the concern of planetary scientists like Alan Stern, Principal Investigator of NASA's New Horizons Mission, who believe Pluto is a planet and IAU's definition is flawed.

In 2006 the National Aeronautics and Space Administration (NASA) sent the New Horizons spacecraft on a nine-and one-half-year-journey to fly by Pluto to learn more about it and the Kuiper Belt. New Horizons reached Pluto on July 14, 2015. It began sending back the first close-up photos ever seen. It was an exciting time for mission scientists and the public.

Imagine how thrilled they were when they saw a large heart-shaped area on Pluto. It sits in a deep valley over 600 miles wide covered with ice and ringed by icy mountains taller than Earth's Rocky Mountains. It was named Tombaugh Regio in honor of Clyde. This heart-shaped region has earned the affection of many people.

The New Horizons spacecraft has flown past Pluto and is exploring the distant Kuiper Belt. When it leaves the Kuiper Belt some time in 2028-2034, it will travel through interstellar space between the stars. Bon Voyage New Horizons! Well done!

Thanks to Alan Stern, Principal Investigator, NASA's New Horizons Mission for his help with this story.

This photo enlarges a portion of Pluto's "heart," showing the icy mountain ranges and plains.

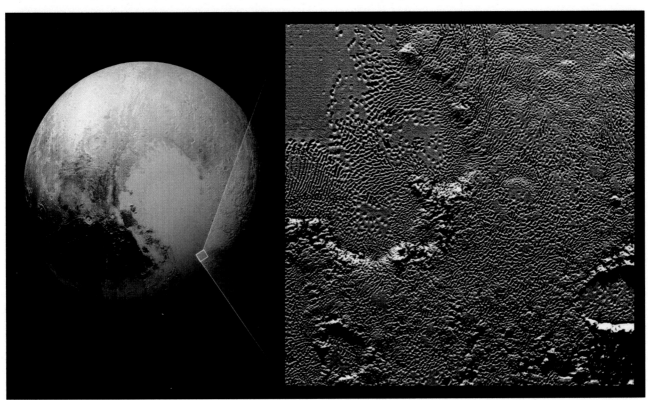

Glossary

Asteroid
Small rocky objects that orbit the sun. Most of the asteroids in our solar system are between Mars and Jupiter.

Astronomy
The study of the sun, moon, stars, planets and other objects in the universe beyond earth's atmosphere.

Astronomer
Scientist who studies space

Blink machine
Used by astronomers to study photographs taken of space by flashing ("blinking") between them to reveal movement of planets.

Dome
Rounded roof of an observatory with movable shutters that house a telescope to study space.

Galaxy
Huge collection of gas, dust and billions of stars and their solar systems held together by gravity. Earth is part of a solar system that is in the Milky Way Galaxy.

Hypothermia
When the body loses heat faster than it can make it and body temperature falls below 95 degrees. It leads to shivering, stiff muscles and sleepiness.

Logbook
A notebook for official records of events or activities.

Observatory
A building that can house a telescope dome to view the night skies.

Star clusters
Groups of stars tied together by gravity. Globular star clusters are ancient, giant star clusters.

Telescope
A tube-like device used by astronomers to see and study distant planets and stars in space.

Threshing machine
Used on farms to separate seeds of grain from its stalks and husks by beating the plants until the seeds fall.

Diane Phelps Budden - Author

Diane Phelps Budden's first children's books were about ravens: *Shade: A Story About a Very Smart Raven* and *The Un-Common Raven: One Smart Bird*, a 2013 panelist pick for Southwest Book of the Year. She presents workshops about self-publishing at libraries and conferences, and volunteers in her local school to help children with reading and writing stories. In her spare time, Diane practices her second love—artmaking. Mother to five and grandmother to five, she lives in Sedona, Arizona, with her supportive husband and many ravens flying overhead. - www.dianephelpsbudden.com

Tanja Bauerle - Designer

Tanja Bauerle is an award-winning children's book illustrator and book designer, who was born in Germany, moved to Australia at age eleven, and now calls Arizona home with her family. Tanja has illustrated picture books and more and is writing and illustrating several of her own projects including an illustrated middle grade historical fiction novel. She runs her own graphic design & branding business and holds a degree in computer animation. Tanja loves sharing her passion for writing & illustrating by teaching workshops to creators of all ages and serves as the Assistant Regional Advisor for the Arizona region of the SCBWI. - www.tanjabauerle.com

Bibliography

Hoyt, William Graves. *Planet X and Pluto*. Tucson, Arizona: The University of Arizona Press, 1980.

Levy, David H. *Clyde Tombaugh: Discoverer of Planet Pluto*. Cambridge, Massachusetts: Sky Publishing Corp., 2006.

McAnulty, Stacy. *Pluto! Not a Planet? Not a Problem!* New York: Henry Holt and Company, 2023

Rigby, H. "The Stars Dipped Down Over Burdette." *Kansas Teacher*, September 1946: 18.

Shindler, Kevin, interview, Lowell Observatory, July 2020 and 2023.

Schindler, Kevin and Grundy, Will. *Pluto and Lowell Observatory: A History of Discovery at Flagstaff*. Charleston, SC: The History Press, 2018.

Scott, Elaine. *When is a Planet Not a Planet?* New York: Clarion Books, 2007.

Stern, Alan, and Grinspoon, David. *Chasing New Horizons: Inside the Epic First Mission to Pluto*. New York: Picador, 2018.

Sweitzer, Paul. "Tombaugh Returns to Flagstaff, Remembers." *The SUN*, Flagstaff, Arizona, March 23, 1980, section A3:1.

The New York Times. "Ninth Planet Discovered on Edge of Solar System; First Found in 84 Years," March 14, 1930, 1,14.

Tombaugh, Alden interview, February 27, 2020.

Tombaugh, Clyde. "My Autobiography." Biographies and Curricula Vitae, 1950s-1980s. NMSU Department of Astronomy, Clyde W. Tombaugh papers. Las Cruces, NM: NMSU Library Archives & Special Collections Department.

Tombaugh, Clyde W. and Moore, Patrick. *Out of the Darkness: The Planet Pluto*. Harrisburg, PA: Stackpole Books, 1980.

Tombaugh, Clyde W. "When I Discovered Pluto," in *Arizona Memories*, eds. Anne Hodges Morgan and Rennard Strickland, 243-253. Tucson, Arizona: University of Arizona Press.

Tombaugh, Clyde W. and Slipher, Vesto M., "13-inch Observation Logbook Volume I, 1929-1930," *Lowell Observatory Archives*, accessed August 29, 2023, https://collectionslowellobservatory.omeka.net/items/show/1538.

"I guess my sister sized me up right. She thinks I discovered a whole new world. I guess I did. How would you feel if you saw a new world giving you the high sign?"

— Clyde W. Tombaugh